GA
CEN(

Novels for Students, Volume 34

Project Editor: Sara Constantakis Rights Acquisition and Management: Beth Beaufore, Sara Crane, Leitha Etheridge-Sims, Barb McNeil Composition: Evi Abou-El-Seoud Manufacturing: Drew Kalasky

Imaging: John Watkins

For product information and technology assistance, contact us at **Gale Customer Support, 1-800-877-4253.**

For permission to use material from this text or product, submit all requests online at www.cengage.com/permissions.

Further permissions questions can be emailed to **permissionrequest@cengage.com** While every effort has been made to ensure the reliability of the information presented in this publication, Gale, a part of Cengage Learning, does not guarantee the accuracy of the data contained herein. Gale accepts no payment for listing; and inclusion in the publication of any organization, agency, institution, publication, service, or individual does not imply endorsement of the editors or publisher. Errors brought to the attention of the publisher and verified to the satisfaction of the publisher will be corrected in future editions.

Gale
27500 Drake Rd.
Farmington Hills, MI, 48331-3535

ISBN-13: 978-1-4144-4172-6
ISBN-10: 1-4144-4172-X
ISSN 1094-3552

This title is also available as an e-book.
ISBN-13: 978-1-4144-4950-0

ISBN-10: 1-4144-4950-X
Contact your Gale, a part of Cengage Learning sales
representative for ordering information.

Printed in the United States of America
1 2 3 4 5 6 7 14 13 12 11 10

Adam Bede

George Eliot

1859

Introduction

The first novel of renowned British Victorian writer George Eliot, *Adam Bede* (1859), is the tragic tale of a love triangle between a dairymaid, a carpenter, and a wealthy young squire. The name George Eliot is misleading; the novelist took this pen name to conceal her female identity, possibly from a culture less inclined to read women writers as seriously as male writers. George Eliot's real name was Mary Anne Evans.

Adam Bede is set in a rural English village, but

the quiet country setting masks turbulent lives. A strong young carpenter named Adam Bede is in love with the beautiful dairymaid Hetty Sorrel and dreams of marrying her. Hetty, a vain and shallow girl, is soon seduced by the young village squire, Arthur Donnithorne. When he leaves her, she reluctantly accepts a proposal from Adam, only to find herself pregnant with Arthur's child. Unable to find a solution to her situation, she abandons her child. The child dies, and Hetty is forever exiled from her home. Adam ends up marrying the gentle and good Dinah, a Methodist preacher, while Arthur Donnithorne struggles to become a better man. The book sensitively depicts the inner lives of these villagers.

Eliot, raised an Evangelical Christian, based her 1859 novel on a story she had heard her Methodist Aunt Samuel tell about how she had preached and redeemed a fallen woman prisoner who was much like Hetty Sorrel. However, Eliot's charming portrait of rural English life comes directly from her own bucolic girlhood. This snapshot of everyday life in a serene country village was already fading when the book was published; the Industrial Revolution was rapidly changing the appearance and culture of British villages. *Adam Bede* was published to not only great critical acclaim but also great popularity among readers nostalgic for bygone days.

George Eliot went on to write classics such as *Silas Marner* and *Middlemarch*. But with her first novel, *Adam Bede*, she manages to create a masterpiece of realism. Each of the characters demonstrates a complexity of thought and action that became the standard for modern novels.

Author Biography

The provocative and unconventional Victorian novelist named George Eliot was born Mary Anne Evans on November 22, 1819. An avid reader, she was the youngest of five children in a family of Evangelical Protestants, and even as a child she taught Sunday school to local children. Her father, on whom her character Adam Bede was based, was a carpenter and land agent in a rural village in Warwickshire, England. It was from her aunt, a Methodist preacher, that Eliot first heard the story that became the novel *Adam Bede*.

When Eliot was sent off to school at age nine, she met an influential teacher named Maria Lewis. Lewis became her spiritual and intellectual mentor for the next fifteen years. A woman of great religious convictions, she did her best to share her faith with her already-devout pupil. She felt Eliot's great intelligence should be nurtured. But Eliot was soon called back home when her mother fell gravely ill.

After her mother's death, Eliot never returned to school; she cared for her beloved father and continued her studies at home. As her education grew, so did her questions about God and faith. She began to break from her childhood religion, much to her father's chagrin.

Two years later she became acquainted with a nonconformist couple, the Brays, who would change the course of her life. Their circle of intellectuals and freethinkers expanded to include the shy but intelligent young woman. She continued to attend church and work on translations of religious work, but inwardly she began to think like her new rationalist friends. Rationalism was a new belief at that time. This philosophy argues that knowledge is acquired by reason, not religious faith.

Soon Eliot stopped attending church, and her distressed father threatened to disown her. They finally agreed that she would attend church, but he could not force her to believe in a faith she no longer held. Their close relationship never recovered. Neither did Eliot's relationship with her old teacher, Maria Lewis.

Following her father's death, Eliot traveled with her friends, the Brays. She then left her small village and moved to London. A married publisher named John Chapman had read and admired her translations and now offered her work. Eventually she became editor of the *Westminster Review.* However, Chapman's interest in her was more than professional. Though photos of Eliot reveal that she was a very plain woman, she was often described as compelling and charming. Her speaking voice was said to have a lovely musical quality. Her relationship with John Chapman was a society scandal.

Soon after, Eliot was introduced to the great love of her life, George Henry Lewes, a writer and critic. Although he too was married and could not divorce, they lived together until his death. It was from him that she took her pen name when she began writing fiction, claiming she wanted to be taken more seriously than women authors were at the time. In 1856 she began writing *Scenes From a Clerical Life*, a collection of stories. Her first novel, *Adam Bede*, was a great popular and critical success. Her realistic depiction of the poor won her many fans.

Over the following years she completed classics such as *The Mill on the Floss* (1860), *Silas Marner* (1861), and *Middlemarch* (1872). With each publication, Eliot's fame spread. She was one of the best-selling novelists of her time.

After Lewes's death in 1878, Eliot grew despondent. She refused to see her friends for a long period, causing concern. However, she agreed to marry her business advisor, John Cross, a man nearly twenty years her junior, in the spring of 1880. Their marriage lasted less than a year; Eliot died in December 1880, from a passing flu, at the age of sixty-one. She is buried next to George Lewes in Highgate Cemetery, England.

Plot Summary

Book 1, Chapter 1: The Workshop

In the opening paragraph of *Adam Bede,* the reader is invited into a rural English woodshop, circa 1799. Adam Bede, a handsome young carpenter, and his kindhearted brother Seth work diligently among the other carpenters. Seth admits that a gentle young Methodist preacher named Dinah has captured his thoughts. He looks forward to hearing her preach that evening. The other workers are disdainful of a woman preacher, and Adam is somewhat disdainful of religion itself. He is also aghast at the way the other carpenters leave the shop the instant the workday is over. A visitor to the village admires his handsome form as he walks toward home.

Book 1, Chapter 2: The Preaching

That same evening, pretty Methodist Dinah preaches to a coolly receptive group of villagers. The villagers are not enthusiastic about Methodist teachings, or women preaching these teachings. However, Dinah is a gifted speaker, and her words about God's love are stirring and simple. She urges all her listeners to think about goodness and piety. Some of the villagers weep at Dinah's preaching, and embrace her despite their non-Methodist leanings.

Book 1, Chapter 3: After the Preaching

After her inspired sermon, Seth takes Dinah home. She is distant, and he feels little encouragement that his love for her is reciprocated. Instead, Dinah tells him she plans to return and preach to the mill town of Snowfield. She regrets leaving her aunt, Mrs. Poyser, and her cousin, Hetty Sorrel. Dinah prays for this young girl, and Seth bemoans his brother, Adam's, attachment to Hetty. Seth bumbles into a declaration of love for the godly Dinah. Dinah is gentle in her refusals, explaining that God will not allow her to marry or have children. She must continue to preach. Seth accepts Dinah's rejection with a heavy heart.

Media Adaptations

- A filmed adaptation of the novel was released in 1918. The six-reeler was produced in England by International Exclusives, Inc. Bransby Williams plays the title role. The film is not available on DVD.

- A BBC television miniseries, starring the popular actress Patsy Kensit, was a great success. It was directed by Giles Foster. It first aired on the BBC in 1991, then aired as part of the PBS anthology *Masterpiece Theatre* in 1992. Iain Glen played the role of Adam Bede. The film is available on DVD in the United States.

Book 1, Chapter 4: Home and Its Sorrows

Adam and Seth's pious mother, Lisbeth, waits for them at home. Their father is a drinker, and in a moment ripe with foreshadowing, Adam discovers that his father has left the house without completing a promised coffin. Adam is annoyed by his father's selfish actions. He angrily sits down to work. Seth attempts to calm his mother, who cries when she thinks of Adam marrying shallow Hetty Sorrel. After they go to sleep, Adam imagines he hears a knock at the door. The villagers believe this means death is arriving. He manages to complete the coffin by the morning, and Seth assists him in bringing it to town. There they find their drowned, drunken father. The discovery fills Adam with bitter regret for his previous conduct.

Book 1, Chapter 5: The Rector

A shift of scenery takes the reader from the simple dwellings of the Bede family to the Broxton Parsonage. The parish clerk enters and tells Reverend Adolphus Irwine that Dinah and the other Methodists are stirring up the villagers. The parson is less upset than curious and resolves to talk to Dinah. He is pleased when his friend Arthur Donnithorne arrives. The dashing Donnithorne is recovering from a war injury. He is the favorite grandson of the town squire, due to inherit wealth and prestige. The parish clerk tells the men the upsetting news that Thias Bede died tragically the night before.

Book 1, Chapter 6: The Hall Farm

Dinah is staying at Hall Farm with her aunt's family. Her aunt, Mrs. Poyser, is plainspoken but sharp-tongued. She is clearly fond of her niece, but remonstrates with her for not marrying Seth Bede and raising a family. Mrs. Poyser uses the arrival of Mr. Irwine and Arthur Donnithorne to complain about the state of their land and property, as she is a tenant of Arthur Donnithorne's grandfather.

Book 1, Chapter 7: The Dairy

Mrs. Poyser shows the gentlemen her dairy, where they find the beautiful Hetty Sorrel working. Arthur Donnithorne is immediately taken with her. They gaze at each other flirtatiously, and the air is electric with their attraction.

Book 1, Chapter 8: A Vocation

Mr. Irwine talks with Dinah, admiring her sweet spirit and religious fervor. Dinah explains that God called to her, and so she answered. She works in a mill in Snowfield, and she yearns to heal those around her from spiritual pain. Mr. Irwine says nothing about Dinah's preaching on the village green. Later, Dinah and her aunt agree that Mr. Irwine is a gentleman. Dinah also tells Mrs. Poyser that Mr. Bede drowned the night before and she is going to go pray with the family. Although Hetty hears this, she is unmoved by Adam's tragic loss.

Book 1, Chapter 9: Hetty's World

Hetty indulges herself in romantic fantasies about Arthur Donnithorne. She knows that solid but unexciting Adam is taken with her, but she vastly prefers the rich Arthur Donnithorne's attentions. Meanwhile, Mr. Irwine advises Arthur Donnithorne not to lead the silly Hetty on, and Arthur Donnithorne protests that he has no intention of doing so.

Book 1, Chapter 10: Dinah Visits

Lisbeth

Lisbeth Bede has spent the day in funeral preparations for her imperfect but now-mourned husband. No one can comfort her. When Dinah arrives, Lisbeth is not open to her ministry. However, Dinah's sincere and loving manner wins her over, as do her words of religious faith. Lisbeth finally embraces her as a daughter. Her grief ebbs with Dinah's care and prayers, and Seth is grateful for her attentions to his mother.

Book 1, Chapter 11: In the Cottage

Adam meets Dinah and thanks her for comforting his mother. He admires Dinah's serene beauty and appreciates his brother's infatuation. Lisbeth asks Adam to work on his father's coffin instead of at the shop in town. She insists that his father would have wanted Adam to do the work independently, and so he finally agrees. Seth arranges to walk Dinah back to Hall Farm. Adam urges his brother to hold on to hope that Dinah will someday accept his love.

Book 1, Chapter 12: In the Wood

Hetty Sorrel arrives at Arthur Donnithorne's estate to learn needlework from his servant, Mrs. Pomfret. He tries, but he cannot resist the urge to see her. He catches up with her as she crosses the woods. She tells him she would like to be a lady's maid, a rank far below his own. He is taken with

Hetty's lovely face, and for a moment he holds her close. But he quickly recovers himself, and rides off with a quick good-bye. Hetty is sad and puzzled by his retreat. Later Arthur Donnithorne resolves to see Hetty once more to make sure she understands that, given their social classes, an attachment would be impossible.

Book 1, Chapter 13: Evening in the Wood

Hetty's girlish heart is still stirred by Arthur's attentions. Mrs. Pomfret, her needlepoint teacher, thinks to herself that Hetty's beauty is not a blessing. Men, she reasons, want a practical wife. Hetty anxiously waits to see if Arthur Donnithorne will cross her path again on her way home. He appears, but his original intention goes awry. Instead, he comforts the weeping girl with a kiss. When he says good-bye, he realizes anew that their connection is impossible. With fresh resolve, he decides to confess to his friend, Mr. Irwine.

Book 1, Chapter 14: The Return Home

Back at the Bedes' house, Lisbeth is very sad to say good-bye to Dinah. She remarks to Adam that he could marry her. Adam shrugs this off, as he is deeply in love with Hetty. Seth takes Dinah back to Hall Farm. Hetty says nothing about Adam's regard for her, or his family's recent loss. When Totty, the

Poysers' little girl, becomes fussy, only Dinah can comfort her. Hetty seems to have no talent with children.

Book 1, Chapter 15: The Two Bed-Chambers

Hetty puts on a pair of earrings and admires her reflection. Just because a woman is beautiful, the narrative asserts, it does not follow that she is good. Hetty's silliness is in sharp contrast to Dinah's piety. Before Dinah goes to sleep, she takes a moment to assure Hetty that she will be there for her if trouble comes. Hetty fearfully rejects Dinah's words.

Book 1, Chapter 16: Links

Arthur Donnithorne is resolved to tell Mr. Irwine about Hetty, but on the way he runs across Adam Bede. The two remember their shared boyhood games, and Arthur Donnithorne urges Adam to accept money to start his own shop. Arthur Donnithorne loses his nerve and does not mention Hetty to Mr. Irwine. Instead, he remarks that a struggle with morals at least implies that the morals are within a man. Mr. Irwine suspects this is about Hetty, but he is too delicate to prompt any confession.

Book 2, Chapter 17: In Which the

Story Pauses a Little

Here the narrator pauses to assure the reader that it is more important to be kind and well loved than to be a great preacher. The town regards Mr. Irwine with greater affection than the previous clergyman. Kindness is more important than intelligence and sophistication.

Book 2, Chapter 18: Church

The Poysers get ready to attend Adam's father's funeral. Hetty is hoping to see Arthur Donnithorne at the service. Adam is distressed by his unkindness to his father. He concentrates on Hetty's beautiful and grave face. She is not, however, thinking about the funeral. She is upset that Arthur Donnithorne has left town for a trip and will not be at the church. She worries that he is already tired of her.

Book 2, Chapter 19: Adam on a Working Day

The next morning the weather is fine. Adam ponders a future with Hetty. He is still unsure if she loves him, and he decides to press her when he goes to the Poyser farm that evening. He knows Mr. Poyser finds him the perfect suitor. The narrator assures the reader that Adam is an unusually good man of his station.

Book 2, Chapter 20: Adam Visits

the Hall Farm

Adam spruces himself up to go to Hall Farm over his mother's objections. He finds the usual bustle at Hall Farm when he arrives. Hetty is flirtatious, and she leads Adam to believe she loves him. She puts a flower in her hair, and Adam expresses his disapproval of her desire to be ornamented. Hetty saucily goes up to her room and returns wearing a Dinah-style Methodist cap, implying that Adam has requested her to look this way. Adam leaves believing Hetty loves him, although she prefers her dreams of a life with Arthur Donnithorne.

Book 2, Chapter 21: The Night-School and the Schoolmaster

Adam meets his night-school teacher and friend Bartle Massey, a confirmed bachelor. He tells Adam about a job managing the squire's fields and offers to put a word in for Adam. Adam accepts, praising his wisdom. The two men part, Massey inviting Adam to a Friday outing.

Book 3, Chapter 22: Going to the Birthday Feast

Everyone is looking forward to Captain Arthur Donnithorne's coming-of-age party. Hetty tries on a pair of gold earrings he has given her, and a locket containing intertwining locks of hair. At the squire's house, the celebration is about to begin. Mr. Irwine tells Arthur that Adam has been offered the position taking care of the squire's lands, and the two men are pleased.

Book 3, Chapter 23: Dinner-Time

Adam Bede and Bartle Massey are invited to eat dinner with the more prosperous villagers. Everyone enjoys dinner, and Adam enjoys gazing at Hetty. He fails to notice that Hetty is impatient with Totty. This does not escape Mary Burge, who hopes Adam sees that she herself has a better temperament. However, when Hetty realizes her rival, Mary Burge, is watching them, she flirts with Adam.

Book 3, Chapter 24: The Health-Drinking

The tenant farmers salute Arthur Donnithorne with birthday speeches and praise. Arthur Donnithorne feels a secret shame about Hetty. However, he decides the flirtation has not been serious. He happily announces Adam's new position. Adam is slightly embarrassed to be the center of attention, but he gamely promises to do well. Arthur Donnithorne turns over a new leaf by ignoring Hetty.

Book 3, Chapter 25: The Games

The party continues with contests and games. Hetty's beauty is remarked upon, which excites Arthur Donnithorne's vanity. A winning girl cries when she is given an ugly dress as a prize. Arthur Donnithorne gives a shiny pocketknife to the boy who wins his race, and some money to the unhappy girl winner. One of the men from Jonathan Burge's carpentry shop dances a rustic dance to great acclaim.

Book 3, Chapter 26: The Dance

The formal dance begins. Hetty longs to dance with her captain. When she reluctantly accepts a dance from Adam, her small cousin Totty pulls the beads that hold her locket. Adam picks up the locket, noting the locks of hair inside. He decides to ignore the situation although Hetty is clearly embarrassed. Arthur Donnithorne makes one final date with Hetty, planning to finally end the relationship. Despite all evidence, Hetty still believes Arthur Donnithorne will marry her.

Book 4, Chapter 27: A Crisis

A few weeks later, Adam has added caring for the squire's fields to his work at the carpentry shop. He believes Hetty is finally falling in love with him. That afternoon, Adam goes to Hall Farm and discovers Hetty and Arthur Donnithorne kissing. He accosts the captain and demands an explanation. Arthur tries to convince Adam that the kiss was a mere thank-you. Adam rejects his words, telling

Arthur that he has stolen Hetty's heart. He knocks him down angrily.

Book 4, Chapter 28: A Dilemma

Adam is afraid he has killed Arthur. He is relieved when Arthur finally awakens, and helps him to an empty cottage. He runs to find brandy. Arthur Donnithorne hides evidence of Hetty and lies about the extent of his relationship. He reluctantly promises to write a good-bye letter and tell her he is rejoining his regiment. He agrees to hand this letter to Adam the next day.

Book 4, Chapter 29: The Next Morning

Arthur Donnithorne is troubled by how Hetty will react to her abandonment. However, he comforts himself that it will lead to a better future for her. He can never marry her, so Adam should be encouraged to do so. He sends Adam the letter with a note admonishing him that Hetty will be devastated. Adam acknowledges that his feelings for Arthur Donnithorne will never recover. He plans to be gentle with Hetty when he speaks with her again.

Book 4, Chapter 30: The Delivery of the Letter

Adam meets the Poysers after church the next

Sunday. While Hetty is relieved that Adam continues to be kind to her, she still fears he will tell her family about her deed. She decides to be secretive about her feelings. Adam tells her with great sensitivity that Arthur Donnithorne does not love her. Hetty blurts out that Adam is wrong. He gives her the letter as proof, but warns her to read it alone. She is shaken by Adam's words, but he hopes there is room in Hetty's heart for him. On the way home, Seth shows Adam a letter from Dinah in Snowfield. Adam urges Seth to see her, assuring him that sometimes women fall in love slowly.

Book 4, Chapter 31: In Hetty's Bed-Chamber

Arthur Donnithorne's letter is as painful to Hetty as Adam promised. The letter explains that while he loved their time together, they can never be man and wife; their class separation is too significant for them to find happiness. Hetty rails against her lover, weeps all night, and in the morning begs her uncle to allow her to leave Hall Farm to become a lady's maid. Her aunt is upset as she sees the desire to leave as disloyal. She calls Hetty a cherry with a stone at the center. Mr. Poyser refuses Hetty's request, suggesting it would be better for her to become Adam's wife. This idea sinks in slowly, but finally Hetty embraces the thought. The important thing is that her life will change.

Book 4, Chapter 32: Mrs. Poyser "Has Her Say Out"

Mrs. Poyser's talents in the dairy have become the talk of the village. This does not escape the old squire. He asks Mrs. Poyser to supply more from her dairy and give over some of the corn farming to another tenant. While Mr. Poyser reacts mildly to the request, his wife is angered and turns the squire out of the house. She is pleased with herself for being honest with their landlord.

Book 4, Chapter 33: More Links

Adam now reaps the rewards of being a fine worker. He has been made a partner in the carpentry shop. In other happy news, Hetty is seemingly more open to his attentions. Adam decides that perhaps Hetty never loved Arthur Donnithorne. The old squire has been thwarted in his plan to produce more dairy products. Mr. Irwine remarks that despite her sharp tongue he admires Mrs. Poyser. Everyone is amused that the old squire was put in his place by one of his tenants.

Book 4, Chapter 34: The Betrothal

When Adam tells Hetty he is to be the new partner at Jonathan Burge's shop, she leaps to the conclusion that he plans to marry Mary Burge. Noting how upset she is, Adam quickly asks her to marry him. Hetty calms and agrees. Her aunt and uncle are well pleased, and there is discussion of where they will live and when they will marry.

Book 4, Chapter 35: The Hidden Dread

Now that they are betrothed, Adam is completely happy. Seth is less happy as he has given up hope of marrying Dinah. Hetty is detached from her wedding plans. She is pregnant with Arthur's child. She contemplates suicide, but realizes she lacks the courage to kill herself. When she gets a letter from Dinah in Snowfield, she decides on a plan. She will tell everyone that she is visiting Dinah, while really she is going to find Arthur Donnithorne. When she weeps, Adam again mistakenly thinks she is attached to him and sad to say good-bye.

Book 5, Chapter 36: The Journey of Hope

After a long and treacherous journey, Hetty finally alights in the town of Windsor where she expects to find Arthur. When she inquires at a local inn, the innkeeper tells her Arthur Donnithorne is in Ireland. Hetty falls to the floor, believing her last hope is gone. The innkeeper quickly figures out her situation, but she is kind to her nonetheless.

Book 5, Chapter 37: The Journey in Despair

As she has little money, Hetty is forced to give up her earrings to pay for staying at an inn. She starts back toward Hall Farm, but she cannot face her aunt and uncle in her condition. Hetty resolves again to kill herself, but once again, she loses her nerve. After a sleepless night in a poor hut, Hetty remembers Dinah's letter and address. She heads pitifully toward Snowfield, thinking that Dinah might still be kind to her.

Book 5, Chapter 38: The Quest

Hetty has now been gone for nearly two weeks, and the Poysers are puzzled as to why she should stay so long. Adam sets off for Snowfield, certain he will return with his bride. But he soon discovers that Hetty never visited Dinah, who left to preach in Leeds before Hetty arrived. The news sends Adam into a tailspin. He secretly suspects she has left him for Arthur Donnithorne. He resolves to find Hetty in Ireland and bring her home, but before he does, he confesses his suspicions to wise Mr. Irwine.

Book 5, Chapter 39: The Tidings

Adam arrives at the parsonage to find Mr. Irwine uncharacteristically upset. He tells Adam he believes Hetty is in prison, accused of killing her own baby. He also tells him Arthur Donnithorne is not in Ireland but on his way back to Hayslope. His grandfather has sent for him. At first Adam rails against Arthur Donnithorne for his seduction. But he calms, remembering he loves Hetty. The two men agree to go speak to the girl in prison in the hope that it is not her.

Book 5, Chapter 40: The Bitter Waters Spread

The two men soon discover that the girl is Hetty, and worse, the evidence is strongly against her. Mr. Irwine returns home, but Adam stays behind, convinced she is innocent of the terrible charges. The next morning, Mr. Irwine awakens to the news that the old squire has died during the night, assuring Arthur Donnithorne's swift return to Hayslope. Meanwhile, Hall Farm is in mourning over the shame of Hetty's actions, and they send for Dinah to come back. Mr. Irwine is worried about Adam. His friend, Mr. Massey, hurries to the town where Hetty is held, in the hope of helping Adam.

Book 5, Chapter 41: The Eve of the Trial

Hetty's trouble seems to have aged Adam, and she refuses to see him or anyone else. Although his friend Mr. Massey urges him, Adam chooses not to attend her trial; he can't bear to see Hetty in the courtroom. When Mr. Irwine comes to visit, he is shocked at Adam's appearance. He tells him the Poysers are in town for the trial, but Dinah has still not been located. Adam talks about vengeance for Arthur Donnithorne's actions, but Mr. Irwine speaks to him gently and Adam finally drops the thought of violence. He ponders whether Dinah's loving ways could have swayed Hetty from her actions.

Book 5, Chapter 42: The Morning of the Trial

Mr. Massey returns from the courtroom with bad news. Hetty will surely be declared guilty of the charges. Mr. Massey tells Adam with some compassion that Hetty looked very alone and without anyone to support her in the courtroom. The prison chaplain is a sharp-faced man without Mr. Irwine's gentleness. Adam shakes off his fears and decides to go to the courtroom after all.

Book 5, Chapter 43: The Verdict

Hetty is the only one who doesn't turn to look at Adam when he enters the courtroom. Like a corpse, all her warmth and humanity seems to have been drained away. A widow testifies she helped Hetty give birth in her home, and a farmer found her dead child not far away. The police found her near her baby the next day. She listens, visibly trembling, to the testimony against her. When the verdict is read, no one is surprised that she is convicted of murder. She is hysterical as she learns she has been sentenced to hang.

Book 5, Chapter 44: Arthur's Return

Arthur Donnithorne happily nears Hayslope, after a very long journey. He knows his grandfather was unpopular, and he believes the villagers will now welcome him as the new squire. He thinks of Hetty, and wonders if he loves her. But while he relishes the memory of her kisses, he is pleased that she is about to marry Adam. However, his good mood is short-lived. When he opens a letter informing him of Hetty's misfortune, he immediately rides off to see her.

Book 5, Chapter 45: In the Prison

Dinah finally arrives at the prison to see Hetty. She meets a man who had been impressed by her preaching in Hayslope, and he turns out to be a magistrate. He permits Dinah to enter Hetty's cell and therefore unlock her heart. At first, Hetty is unresponsive. But after listening to Dinah's soft words about God's love, she finally tells her that she did abandon her child. She thought it the only way out of her dilemma. The two girls hold each other, and Hetty is comforted although she still fears her sentence. She tells Dinah she hears her dead child crying for her.

Book 5, Chapter 46: The Hours of Suspense

Adam agrees to go see Hetty on the day she will be executed. Ironically, it was to be their wedding day. Dinah is with her, and she tells Adam that God has not forsaken Hetty. She plans to be a source of strength for the condemned girl. Hetty begs Adam to forgive her for hurting him, and they say a mournful good-bye to each other. Dinah encourages Hetty to forgive her lover too. In this way, she tells her cousin, God will extend forgiveness to Hetty.

Book 5, Chapter 47: The Last Moment

At the gallows, it seems all hope is lost. Dinah and Hetty pray together in front of a quiet crowd awaiting Hetty's execution. Just then, Arthur Donnithorne gallops forward, waving a stay of execution. Hetty will not die that day after all.

Book 5, Chapter 48: Another Meeting in the Wood

The next night, Adam is back in Hayslope, as is Arthur Donnithorne. The two meet in the same cottage where Adam took Arthur Donnithorne after their fight. They are somber together, each having suffered. Arthur Donnithorne plans to rejoin the military, but he urges Adam to stay in the village. He allows that Dinah was wonderful to Hetty, and he gives Adam a fine watch in reward. Adam admits he is perhaps too hard on people. The two shake hands and part as friends. Hetty's death sentence has been commuted to exile.

Book 6, Chapter 49: At the Hall Farm

It is more than a year later. Mr. Poyser believes Adam will soon be the sole owner of the carpentry shop. Dinah is at last planning to return to Snowfield, as she feels the poor there have more need of her than the Poysers. She feels she must reject the ease of her lifestyle at the farm. Adam hears she plans to return to Snowfield and says he trusts she will always follow the right path. At this, Dinah mysteriously leaves Adam and the Poysers to their talk. When she returns, Adam asks her to come back with him and visit his mother.

Book 6, Chapter 50: In the Cottage

Dinah asks if Adam has heard anything of Arthur Donnithorne, and Adam tells her he is still upset about Hetty's disgrace. Dinah compares him to Esau from the Bible, and talks of him with sympathy. When they discuss Dinah's plan to go back to Snowfield, Adam urges her to stay and marry his brother. The words send Dinah into an unusually emotional state, and Adam is surprised. Lisbeth and Seth note that Dinah does not seem herself. Dinah tells Lisbeth that her emotions will pass. The next morning, Dinah meets Adam cleaning up his workshop, and feels a thrill at his deep voice. Adam asks her if she is upset with him, but she tells him she knows she is a sister to him. The narrator suggests Dinah is in love.

Book 6, Chapter 51: Sunday Morning

Lisbeth, who is very attached to Dinah, wails at the thought of her leaving town yet again. Lisbeth believes Dinah loves Adam, and that she might stay if Adam decided to marry her. Her words are hurtful to Seth, who still loves Dinah. He declares the two are like siblings, but he would still be happy if they found a match. Lisbeth decides to speak with Adam, and he quickly warms to the idea of the good and gentle Dinah as his wife. Seth reassures Adam that he would not object to the match; however, he believes she will never accept Adam's proposal.

Book 6, Chapter 52: Adam and Dinah

There is good news and bad news for Adam that Sunday. The good news is that Dinah returns his love for her. The bad news is that she has decided to return to Snowfield and remain single. She would no longer have the poor as her priority if she married and had children of her own. Adam attempts to argue, but she tells him she will go back to Snowfield and await God's word. Meanwhile, Mrs. Poyser claims she was not surprised by Adam and Dinah's love. Everyone enjoys the fine day, and the narrator calls attention to how important a day of leisure is in busy lives.

Book 6, Chapter 53: The Harvest

Supper

The harvest is done, and to celebrate, the Poysers invite their field-workers and farmers to a special dinner. Adam is there, but Dinah has returned to Snowfield as she promised. However, the mood is still jubilant. Mr. Poyser is proud of his offerings, songs are sung, and a new spirit of renewal is in the air. Mr. Massey, Adam's schoolteacher friend, pokes fun at his love for women. They both agree that Mrs. Poyser's wit is admirable.

Book 6, Chapter 54: The Meeting on the Hill

Adam yearns to see Dinah. He decides to travel to Snowfield. On his journey, he remembers the beautiful Hetty, and he feels a pang at her memory. However, this experience may have paved the way to a deeper love for Dinah, and he can come to her with a full heart. When Dinah sees him waiting for her, she tells him their love is so true God must want them to be together. She agrees to marry him, and they share a tender first kiss.

Book 6, Chapter 55: Marriage Bells

Finally, it is Adam and Dinah's wedding day, a time of true joy for both. Their union pleases the entire village. Dinah wears a plain gray dress, but her pretty face glows with happiness. Although Mr. Irwine remembers the great sorrow Adam has suffered, he is especially happy that he can give this great news to Arthur Donnithorne, who has never returned to Hayslope.

Epilogue

The novel ends with a view of Adam and Dinah's happy marriage. It is nearly ten years later, and they are the parents of two children. Adam is also sole owner of the carpentry shop. Seth lives with Adam's family and the children are fond of him. Adam tells Dinah that Arthur Donnithorne is finally returning to Hayslope. He's been very ill, but is expected to recover. Hetty died just before she would have been allowed to return to her home. The three family members briefly discuss how women are no longer allowed to preach. Adam is in favor of this, but Dinah clearly is not. However, this is a small shadow over their great happiness.

Characters

Adam Bede

Adam Bede is a young and handsome carpenter, much admired in the village of Hayslope for his intelligence and industry. He is a good man to his friends and family, but he is also somewhat rigid and unable to see other perspectives. Eventually he becomes the steward of the lands, a very desirable position, through his boyhood camaraderie with the squire's grandson, Arthur Donnithorne.

Adam works at the Burges' carpentry shop with his brother, Seth, and he dreams of marrying the beautiful Hetty Sorrel. However, his love for Hetty is based primarily on her beauty, not her goodness. They become betrothed, but when Hetty is arrested for murdering her child and sent into exile, Adam turns to Dinah Morris. He becomes a much more compassionate man through his experience with Hetty, and eventually he and Dinah fall in love. When the novel ends, Adam is the owner of the carpentry shop. Dinah and Adam are parents of two children, and very happy.

Lisbeth Bede

Lisbeth is Adam and Seth Bede's mother. She is widowed when her husband, Thias Bede, drowns during a drunken spree. This causes Lisbeth much grief, although he was not always a good husband to her. Lisbeth appears to be very fragile, but actually she is quite astute. She realizes Dinah and Adam should marry before they do, and she guesses correctly that Dinah will not be interested in marrying her younger son, Seth. While she spends much of the novel in tears, she is often comforted by the preaching and soft words of Dinah, whom she loves like a daughter.

Seth Bede

Adam's younger brother, Seth, is good-natured but he lacks the steel of Adam's personality. The other men in the woodshop poke fun at him. While he is a gentle and caring man, he is also a bit of a daydreamer. Like Dinah Morris, he is a Methodist, and he loves hearing her preach. Although he declares his love for her early in the novel, Dinah rejects him. His sweet personality holds no grudges, and he continues to be her supporter and friend. When Adam marries her, he is happy for both of them. He is also in favor, unlike Adam, of woman preachers. At the end of the novel Seth has remained a single man. In fact, he is living happily with Dinah, Adam, and their children.

Thias Bede

The drunkard father of Adam and Seth dies tragically by drowning. While he was once an industrious carpenter, over time he has become a drinker. He represents a realistic portrait of an alcoholic in this time period. His sons discover his body while they are taking a coffin to town. His funeral is attended by much of Hayslope. Thias Bede is sincerely mourned by his wife and his sons, despite his drunkenness and his other faults.

Mr. Jonathan Burge

Mr. Burge owns the carpentry shop where Adam and Seth work in Hayslope. His daughter, Mary Burge, is in love with Adam. Although Adam marries Dinah and not his daughter, Mr. Burge decides to give his shop to Adam anyway. He tries to replace him but can never find another carpenter of Adam's ability.

Mary Burge

Mary is the daughter of the master carpenter in town, and her love for Adam Bede remains unrequited. She is a quiet and plain girl. She spurs Hetty Sorrel to flirt with Adam, an act that results in Adam and Hetty's eventual engagement.

Arthur Donnithorne

The weak-minded but handsome young captain is the rich heir to his grandfather's lands and estate. He is much admired in Hayslope, but his passion for Hetty Sorrel proves to be his undoing. Arthur wants everyone to like him, and so he often takes the easy way out of his troubles. He avoids telling Hetty

Sorrel that he will never marry her until it is too late, and he neglects to confess to his friend and parson, Mr. Irwine, about his relationship with her.

However, by the end of the novel, Arthur has learned some important lessons. He saves Hetty from the gallows with a last-minute reprieve, and he never forgets he was the instrument of her sorrow. He also suffers through illness and despair, eventually returning to Hayslope a changed man. His kindnesses are also noted, not only to Adam Bede, but also to the other villagers. He awards the young winner of a race a pocketknife, and gives another a gift of money.

Squire Donnithorne

The aged squire is the grandfather of the dashing Arthur Donnithorne. He is extremely disliked in Hayslope, and a very bad landlord. When he asks Mrs. Poyser to give up rich farmlands and spend more time producing goods in the dairy, she publicly berates him to everyone's amusement. He dies a bitter old man.

Mr. Irwine

The lifelong bachelor Mr. Irwine is a shining example of a helpful clergyman. Eliot claims he is not brilliant but is, more importantly, well loved. Mr. Irwine is never judgmental about his flock, and he treats Hetty Sorrel with compassion. While he is a good friend with Arthur Donnithorne, he calls him to task for his actions toward Hetty. He also makes sure Adam finds Hetty in prison, and he encourages his friend Bartle Massey to take care of him during this difficult period.

A nonviolent man, he manages to talk Adam Bede out of further conflict with Arthur. He is also not upset that Dinah Morris preaches in the town square. Mr. Irwine brings his balanced wisdom to all situations in the novel that call for the voice of reason.

Bartle Massey

Bartle Massey is a disabled schoolmaster and a bachelor who pokes fun at Adam's love affairs. However, he stays beside him when Hetty is arrested, proving himself a very good friend. For Bartle, his female dog Vixen is a much better companion than any woman. Adam is one of the best students at his night school.

Dinah Morris

Dinah is a gentle and sweet-natured Methodist preacher. She is Mrs. Poyser's niece, and often visits the family at Hall Farm in Hayslope, where she preaches in the village square. When she is at home in Snowfield, she works at a mill. She is compassionate and helpful to those in need, and ministers to both Lisbeth Bede and Hetty Sorrel in their darkest hours. Seth Bede falls in love with her early in the novel, but she tells him she can never marry, as preaching is her calling. Later she belies those words by falling in love with his brother, Adam, and raising a family with him. Although her modest dress and demeanor are very different from those of her cousin, Hetty Sorrel, she is also described as very pretty. When Hetty is in prison, Dinah comes to her and begs her to confess so that she might feel God's forgiveness. She does, and faces her death bravely, although her sentence is commuted to exile. Dinah's modesty and goodness are apparent to everyone in the village, including Mr. Irwine, the village pastor.

Mr. Poyser

Martin Poyser is an easygoing, talented farmer and a happy man. He often worries about his flighty niece, Hetty, and encourages her to marry the admirable young carpenter, Adam. He is fond of his family, and is greatly upset at Hetty Sorrel's trial.

Mrs. Poyser

Witty and intelligent, Mrs. Poyser is a plain-speaking woman who expects a great deal from her family, although she spoils her youngest child, Totty. She is also compassionate when her niece Hetty gets into trouble. She is renowned in Hayslope for having the courage to speak up to the old squire when he crosses her, and she enjoys showing off her well-run dairy operation.

Hetty Sorrel

Hetty is a beautiful but shallow young peasant girl. She is very vain, and likes finery, although her social status is low. Her uncle is Mr. Poyser, and she works in Mrs. Poyser's dairy. She is also learning the skills of being a lady's maid, and she enjoys the attentions of Adam Bede and other young men. However, she has dreams of becoming the wife of Arthur Donnithorne, the grandson of the town squire. Although he falls in love and seduces her, he eventually tells her they can never marry. After Arthur leaves with his regiment, Hetty reluctantly accepts a proposal from Adam, feeling it will change her life for the better. However, before the marriage can take place, Hetty learns she is pregnant with Arthur's child. She runs off hoping to find him, and when she fails, she abandons her newborn child in a field. This leads to her exile, and eventually, her death. She dies before she can return to her home.

Colonel Towley

The magistrate at Hetty's prison remembers Dinah Morris from her sermon as he rode through Hayslope. Later he allows Dinah to enter Hetty's cell to pray with her.

Themes

Appearance

The appearance of both the countryside and characters makes for a driving theme in *Adam Bede.* Although Hetty Sorrel is a peasant girl, she feels her beauty lends her higher aspirations. Rather than being satisfied with a life with a good man like Adam, she yearns to be a lady and the wife of Arthur Donnithorne. Her appearance, however, is deceptive. Both her suitors feel she is kind and sweet because they each believe that goodness is connected to a lovely face.

Hetty is clearly a silly and frivolous girl. Still, Adam supposes she will make a fine mother and good wife. Actually, Hetty actively dislikes children and is only truly interested in Adam when she is left without any recourse. Adam is not the only one fooled by Hetty's pretty face; Arthur Donnithorne believes Hetty is in love with him, instead of with the status he could bring her if he married her.

Dinah, on the other hand, dresses modestly and does not possess Hetty's lush beauty. However, her simple prettiness shines more brightly when her character is revealed as strong and honest. Appearances, Eliot implies, are not what they may seem; it is best for people to look within, and not without. This also holds true when Hetty trusts that Arthur Donnithorne will marry her because he looks upstanding to the community. Once again, looks are deceptive. Despite his stalwart appearance, Arthur is a coward who weasels out of confessing his time with Hetty to Mr. Irwine and writes a farewell letter to Hetty only after Adam beats him. Arthur is not what he appears to be either.

Topics for Further Study

- The village of Hayslope is described as a beautiful place, full of fields and meadows. The village might be called a character in the book, down to the flapping of butterfly wings on a tree. Research what a small rural village at this time might have looked like, and then re-create it using cardboard and paint to make the houses and lands.

- George Eliot wrote, "Our deeds determine us, as much as we determine our deeds." How does this relate to Hetty Sorrel's actions? Research some historic examples of how people have been fairly or unfairly judged for their deeds. Then write a persuasive essay supporting either side of the issue, providing reasons and examples for your opinion.

- George Eliot was actually a woman named Mary Anne Evans. She took the pen name of George Eliot to hide her gender from the literary world. Does knowing the gender of a writer affect your reading of a novel? Research other writers who wrote under the name of a different gender, and discuss your findings in an essay.

- Hetty is exiled to another country after her sentence is commuted. Although it is never stated, the country is probably Australia, which served as a penal colony for many years. Read about the history of Australia and convicts. Write a story about what Hetty's life might have been like after she was exiled to this unfamiliar land.

- Nineteenth-century literature often features cautionary tales of young peasant women like Hetty who are seduced and betrayed by upper-class men. Thomas Hardy's *Tess of the d'Urbervilles* (1891) is a famous example. Director Roman Polanski adapted the book for a 1979 film called *Tess.* Watch the film, then write a paper in which you compared Tess to Hetty and address whether you think young women today face the same kinds of perils as Tess and Hetty.

The beauty of the English countryside outside Hayslope is also deceptive. Although it is lovely and peaceful, with a noted quiet charm, the setting conceals the turbulent lives of the inhabitants. The countryside is also the scene of Hetty and Arthur's passionate embrace. When Hetty abandons her child, she does so in the midst of beautiful rural lands. Eliot seems to be urging readers to look deeper below the surface of the characters and their villages.

Family

Family ties play a key role in *Adam Bede*. "Family likeness," George Eliot writes, "has often a deep sadness in it. Nature, that great tragic dramatist, knits us together by bone and muscle, and divides us by the subtler web of our brains; blends yearning and repulsion; and ties us by our heart-strings to the beings that jar us at every movement."

In these short sentences, she defines another strong theme: while the love and connection of family pulls the characters together, it also leads to despair.

When Thias Bede drowns early in the novel, his two sons are left to comfort their grieving mother. His father's passing also reminds Adam of his own less-than-wonderful qualities. It reveals he was often unkind and judgmental to his parents, and he struggles to be a better person when his father is gone. Lisbeth Bede can barely function without her husband, and she tries to draw her sons closer to her, even suggesting that Adam marry Dinah, Seth's longtime love.

Hetty's misdeeds also tear apart her family ties. She decides she cannot face her family in her condition, leading to her decision to abandon her child in a field. Her uncle, Mr. Poyser, is bereft at her trial and weeps at her sentence. Dinah returns from afar to hear her confession and accompany her to the gallows.

However, familial love can also be transformative. Seth embraces his brother's marriage to a woman whom he himself loved, and Mrs. Poyser does not judge Hetty for her actions. Although at the beginning of the novel Mrs. Poyser is hard on her family, she is surprisingly warm and accepting of Hetty's troubles. Family can be both blessing and curse for Eliot's characters.

Style

Realism

Realism refers to a type of fiction that depicts life as it is, without romanticizing or glossing over unappealing or unattractive elements. Authors who write in this style often focus on ordinary people, illuminating the characteristics that make everyone distinct and special.

George Eliot is considered one of the first novelists who wrote realistic fiction. This was a distinct change in tone from that of earlier writers. By the early part of the eighteenth century, many Writers wrote in the Romantic style. Novels written in the Romantic style tended to celebrate the world as beautiful and often used literature as an escape rather than an examination of everyday life. Characters in Romantic novels put imagination and feelings above measured thought.

Realism rejected these ideas, proposing that literature should be a conduit for observing the true inner framework of society. Most writers of this style also rejected overly dramatic or sensational events, preferring that characters make realistic decisions about situations. Realism emphasized humanism, a philosophy upholding reason above religious beliefs.

Hence, the decisions characters make are

complex, often weighing an ethical or moral problem. While decisions have consequences, it is possible to argue both sides of the issue. Realistic novels are also objective and withhold judgment, despite depicting sordid lives or choices.

Many of these novels invoked the real language or dialect of the characters they portray. Middle-class readers were given insight into the struggles of the poor, and their own struggles as well.

Hetty Sorrel is a good example of a realistic character. Although she is beautiful, she is also described as shallow and materialistic. Yet her desire to have a wider life is understandable, and her family and friends are sympathetic to the desperation she feels before she abandons her child. Adam Bede is another example. He is both strong and enterprising, yet he is also unyielding and stubborn. Each of these characters behaves with the complexity of real people, struggling with the pain and problems of an ordinary life.

The Industrial Revolution

George Eliot wrote at a time when England's traditional agricultural economy was rapidly becoming replaced by industrialization. As the population grew and became richer, they wanted more available goods. Factories were established to fill this demand, and the population shifted from rural to city life. Growing towns meant larger labor pools were available to work in new factories.

Many young people left their farms to work in factories. These often were located where poverty was high. Poverty meant a high number of available workers. Their lives were hard, as they lived in shabby housing and worked long hours. Factory owners controlled many aspects of their workers' lives, often owning the poor housing. The conditions of the towns and factories were unsanitary and without laws to govern the conditions.

Compare & Contrast

- **1800s:** Hetty Sorrel is disappointed in her hopes of marrying Arthur Donnithorne. In eighteenth-century England, a rich landowner and a dairymaid could not be married and accepted by society.

Today: In 1986, Sarah Ferguson, a commoner, married Prince Andrew at Westminster Abbey. No longer is anyone in England barred from marrying whom they please because of divisions of wealth or property.

- **1800s:** Mrs. Poyser is incensed by the old squire's desire that she give up part of her land. In that time, farmers leased the land they worked. The owner of the land could decide to evict them if the crop failed or they felt the land could be better worked by another farmer.

  Today: Most modern-day farmers are owner-operators of their farms. They use computers and technical equipment to raise a large variety of crops.

- **1800s:** Dinah Morris is a Methodist preacher in *Adam Bede.* Female Methodist preachers were not uncommon in the middle and late 1700s. However, by the end of the novel, she has been forced to stop preaching. The Methodist church barred women from preaching in 1803.

  Today: Fifteen Protestant denominations regularly ordain women as ministers.

As a result of these conditions, many epidemics spread, including cholera. It was many years before an outcry over public health led to stronger laws and better conditions for the poor. The character of Dinah Morris in *Adam Bede* is not only a preacher, she is also a mill worker. George Eliot describes the town of Snowfield where the factory is located as a dismal place, where the poor needed her support and compassion. Dinah, in fact, must steel herself to go back to this work.

Realistic novels such as *Adam Bede* surged in popularity during this time period. Readers felt books describing the rise of factory towns and the squalid lives of factory workers accurately and movingly represented their own struggles. The nostalgic depiction of a vanishing rural life also may have led to the novel's immense popularity.

Women in Early Methodism

In *Adam Bede*, Dinah Morris is an inspirational and gifted Methodist preacher who goes to the village green to spread the word of God. She is also representative of the great evangelical revival movement that began in the early 1700s in both Great Britain and the United States.

Methodism was one of the primary new faiths of this movement. At a time when many churches preached about a wrathful God, Methodism took a gentler path. The church urged participants in services to understand God's love and guidance. From the beginning, women played an important role in this new church.

In the early years, Methodist leaders encouraged people of both genders to embrace their spiritual life. Famous women Methodist leaders included Jane Cooper and Ann Cutler, who were later revered for their work. Women also led Sunday school, visited the infirm and elderly, and often played a vital supporting role in their husband's ministries. These roles were encouraged within the church.

However, Methodism also encouraged the controversial practice of allowing females to preach publicly. In the mid-1700s, women went from enthusiastically welcoming new converts to gospel preaching and gathering. This was a shocking development for many, as the Church of England did not allow women to be ordained until the twentieth century.

But the situation soon changed. The Methodist church began discouraging the many women preachers who had sprung up in towns across the country. By the turn of the century, women were restricted from preaching to men. At the end of *Adam Bede,* an allusion is made to this when Dinah reveals she has been forced to stop preaching in the village. Some women, however, ignored the ban and continued to lead gospel readings. Many were responsible for converting thousands of parishioners.

In 1910, women Methodist ministers were finally welcomed back to the pulpit, and still later, they were granted equal status with male preachers.

Critical Overview

George Eliot was an unknown literary magazine editor when *Adam Bede* was published in 1859. With the publication of her first novel she quickly became revered with both critics and readers. Reviews of Eliot's debut were glowing.

An unnamed reviewer in the *Atlantic Monthly* lauded the work, saying, "*Adam Bede* is remarkable, not less for the unaffected Saxon style which upholds the graceful fabric of the narrative, and for the naturalness of its scenes and characters."

The influential Geraldine Jewsbury called *Adam Bede* "a novel of the highest class. Full of quiet power, without exaggeration and without any strain after effect, it produces a deep impression on the reader, which remains long after the book is closed."

Eliot's subsequent novels were also well received by critics, particularly her novel *Middlemarch*, considered by many to be her most accomplished work. However, some critics felt the books she wrote late in life were less successful and far more heavy-handed.

However, early feminists applauded the way Eliot addressed the fate of women, leading to a new vogue for Eliot's fiction in the early twentieth century. Later feminists also heralded her work, as it contemplated the role of women and questioned the nature of society and these roles.

It is undisputed that Eliot enjoyed great popularity during her lifetime. Her books were widely read and circulated. Eliot's prestige led her from poor literary editor to wealthy celebrity in a few short years. She is still considered one of the prominent writers of the Victorian age.

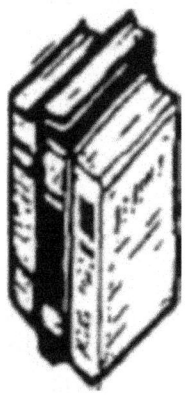

What Do I Read Next?

- *Middlemarch* (1872) is often considered to be George Eliot's masterpiece. Eliot tells the tale of social life in provincial England while recounting the unhappy and ill-fated marriage of a young doctor. Like her other novels, Eliot accurately and devastatingly depicts the social pitfalls and class system of her time.

- The Eliot novel *Silas Marner* (1861) also deals with the theme of status and family in Victorian England. When a miserly Silas Marner discovers an abandoned child and raises her, a community that had once rejected him embraces him. He also learns that love is more important than money.

- The classic *Tess of the d'Urbervilles* (1891) by Thomas Hardy also examines the life of a young woman who falls from grace. Tess, who gives birth to a child named Sorrow, is yet another victim of Victorian morality in this much-filmed novel. Often called a masterpiece of realistic fiction, Hardy's masterpiece is a worthy successor to George Eliot's work.

- Never the most popular of Jane Austen's domestic novels, *Mansfield Park* (1814) is the most complex study of mores and manners of Regency England. Fanny Price is sent away from her childhood home to live with her rich relatives at a large manor house. She falls in love with her cousin, but is considered unsuitable given her social status. However, Fanny's essential goodness prevails. Critics have decried the oddly happy ending that transpires.

- *Great Expectations* (1861) by Eliot's great fan and contemporary, Charles Dickens, truly defines the Victorian novel for some readers. Young Pip falls in love with the cold but beautiful Estella—a heartbreaker who resembles Hetty Sorrel in her desire to climb up the social ladder —but sees his love unrequited for many years. The novel was first published in the popular serial form in 1860 to great acclaim.

- Eric Hobsbawm's acclaimed *Industry and Empire: The Birth of the Industrial Revolution,* first published in 1968, provides a readable, engaging survey of the vast changes brought about in British society by the industrial revolution, which began just before the time in which *Adam Bede* is set.

Sources

"*Adam Bede* by George Eliot," in *The Atlantic Monthly,* Vol. 4, No. 24, October 1859, pp. 521-522.

Blaser, Kent, "John Wesley and the Women Preachers of Early Methodism," in *The Historian,* March 22, 1993, http://www.accessmylibrary.com/search?q=John+Wesley+and+the+Women+Preachers (accessed November 3, 2009.

Eliot, George, *Adam Bede,* Penguin, 2008. Gates, Sarah, "The Sound of the Scythe Being Whetted: Gender, Genre, and Realism in *Adam Bede,*" in *Studies in the Novel,* March 22, 1998, http://www.accessmylibrary.com/search/?q=The+Sound+of+the+Scythe (accessed November 3, 2009).

Jewsbury, Geraldine, "Adam Bede, George Eliot" (review date 1859), in Vol. 89 of *Nineteenth-Century Literary Criticism,* edited by Juliet Byington and Suzanne Dewsbury, The Gale Group, 2001, http://www.enotes.com/nineteenth-century-criticism/adam-bede-george-eliot/geraldine-jewsbury-review-date-1859 (accessed November 3, 2009).

Lamb, John B., "To Obey and Trust: Adam Bede and the Politics of Deference," in *Studies in the Novel,* September 22, 2002,

http://www.accessmylibrary.com/search?
q=To+Obey+and+Trust (accessed November 3,
2009).

Lampman, Jane, "Women Clergy Bring a New
Sensibility to an Old Calling," in *Christian Science
Monitor,* July 19, 2006.

Mitchell, Rebecca N., "Learning to Read:
Interpersonal Literacy in *Adam Bede,*" in *Papers on
Language and Literature,* March 22, 2008,
http://www.accessmylibrary.com/search?
q=Learning+to+Read%3A+Interpersonal+Literacy
(accessed November 3, 2009).

Uglow, Nathan, "George Eliot: *Adam Bede,*" in *The
Literary Encyclopedia,* March 21, 2002,
http://www.litencyc.com/php/sworks.php?
rec=true&UID=6852 (accessed November 3, 2009).

Wojtczak, Helena, "Women's Status in Mid 19th-
Century England: A Brief Overview,"
http://www.hastingspress.co.uk/history/19/overview,
(accessed November 3, 2009).

Further Reading

Hellerstein, Erna O., Leslie P. Hume, and Karen M. Offen, eds., *Victorian Women: A Documentary Account of Women's Lives in Nineteenth-Century England, France and the United States,* Stanford University Press, 1981.

> This account of women's lives in the time of George Eliot offers a variety of examples of famous women and how they were raised.

Brontë, Emily, *Wuthering Heights,* Barnes and Noble Classics, 1985.

> A classic of Romantic writing, the story of Heathcliff and Cathy also offers insights into a class system and the need to marry wealth that often proved tragic for women of that time.

Vicinus, Martha, ed., *Suffer and Be Still: Women in the Victorian Age,* Indiana University Press, 1973.

> A collection of essays from both feminist scholars and historians.

Lightning Source UK Ltd.
Milton Keynes UK
UKHW020614151022
410492UK00013B/845